Writing Prompts Gone *Wild*

£ 2.49

C000091907

To mother and father:

*You're not still mad I gave up
on that medical degree,
are you?*

Prompts Gone Wild
3340 Dewdney Trunk Road
Port Moody, BC, Canada, V3H 2E3
www.promptsgonewild.com

Copyright © 2020 Aaron Barry

First printing edition 2020

All rights reserved. No part of this publication may be reproduced, distributed, or transmitted in any form or by any means, including photocopying, recording, or other electronic or mechanical methods, without the prior written permission of the publisher, except in the case of brief quotations embodied in critical reviews and certain other non-commercial uses permitted by copyright law. For permissions or press and publicity requests, write to the author at promptsgonewild@gmail.com.

ISBN: 978-1-7771927-0-9

Book design by Matt Windsor (thedesigngarden.co.uk)
Author photo by Connor Murphy
Illustrations by @lycheetinii

Printed by Amazon KDP

#promptsgonewild

Writing Prompts Gone Wild

Aaron Barry

Dear depraved wordsmith,

Let's face it—you're a bad person.

Despite your best efforts to remedy that fact—and I'm sure you really have tried everything—you just can't seem to get rid of those niggling moral deficiencies. But despair not. I'm not here to tell you to change or be better. No, I'm here to tell you to embrace the fucked up individual that you are.

In this twisted tome, you'll find writing prompts specifically designed to allow you to indulge in your most sinful fantasies. If you've ever wanted to spend an afternoon with a young Hitler, ponder the sexual proficiency of robots, pen R-rated sonnets in perfect iambic pentameter, or add everyone's favourite Christian, Archbishop Kanye West, to "The Good Book," here's your chance.

So, break out that pen or that set of typing sticks you call fingers, and let's get to it. Consider me your spiritual guide, the Virgil to your debauched Dante, as we traverse topics unfit for the kind-at-heart. Let's laugh, love, and learn together, you little heathen, you!

Enjoy!

How to Use This Book:

Solo
Open book. Read prompt. (Please tell me you can read.) Let creative juices flow. Write. Sound good? Feel free to use whichever style or form you like, unless otherwise specified.

Group
For a real challenge, grab some friends (if you have any) and set a timer for fifteen minutes or your desired duration. Select a prompt at random and have everyone write on it separately (or together if you want a circlejerk exercise). When the time runs out, compare your responses and vote on which entry you think is the funniest. And don't vote for yourself, dude. No one likes that shit.

Rewrite a BDSM scene from *Fifty Shades of Grey*,[1] but make it unbearably PG.

SPANK ME IN MY DREAMS

---

[1] Go ask your lonely aunt for more info on this one if it doesn't ring a bell. She'll know *all* about it.

As an agoraphobic, paranoid schizophrenic, bipolar, ADD, hyper-maniac OCD sufferer, it's sometimes difficult to get out of bed. But when you do, my god, it's fucking hilarious...

The abortion didn't work.

In fact, you now have a new problem to deal with...

...they somehow managed to *add* a fetus.

Finally!

The Trump Administration has recognized you for your impeccable ability to express yourself in 280 characters or fewer. They'd like you to handle his Twitter account while he's away on a golfing trip or some shit. Your first task: levy criticism at your most hated politician.[2]

---

[2] Donald Trump / Joe Biden

Your character is a lot like a James Bond villain—minus the monocle, the money, and the exotic pussy.[3]

Their next dastardly plot: steal a fully-loaded corndog from their local 7-Eleven store.

---

[3] Cat. Exotic pussy cat.

Your train's full of zombies. But, instead of sporting putrefying flesh, mangled teeth, and a marked disregard for privacy, these ones spend their time staring at their phones, humming popular songs, and vaping.

Write a zombie apocalypse story where you have to defend yourself against hoards of the Gen Z undead.

Look in the mirror.

Describe what you see.

On the *inside*.

And being the raging narcissist that you clearly are, refer to yourself in the third-person the whole time.

Foreign object.

Bodily orifice.

Ambulance.

Confused doctors.

Concerned parents.

Explain.

Your best friend is thinking of committing suicide. How do you push them over the edge?

Write your conversation in text form.[4]

I'M GOING THROUGH A RLY TOUGH TIME RN...I DON'T KNOW IF I CAN GET THROUGH THIS... I FEEL SO LOW...

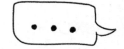

---

[4] I'd be shocked if you didn't know how to do this.

There's nothing quite like hitting someone with a nasty burn. Our boy Billy Shakespeare was the best at roasting fools in his plays.

Let's take a page out of his book and write some sick insults in perfect iambic pentameter.[5]

---

[5] You know, that tricky little rhythmic pattern that used to get your teacher all hot and bothered.[5a]

[5a] Iambic pentameter makes use of five units, each comprised of one unstressed and one stressed syllable. (For the mathematically disinclined: that's ten syllables per line.) It goes a little somethin' like this:

we HATE to READ aBOUT these OLD white MEN

da-DA da-DA da-DA da-DA da-DA

Give 'er the old Quentin Tarantino and rewrite a historical event of your choosing.

Get as fantastical (and bloody) as you like.

Write a story that concludes
with the following line:

"Jesus looked good in
sunglasses…
Almost too good."

After being oozed on by a radioactive slug, your character develops a sad, sad superpower: *Depressive ultra-instinct.*

Write a story about how they use this curiously morose super ability.

Your entire family is at the hospital. A relative is about to pass away.

Your dad is capable of speaking only in dad jokes.[6]

It's *awkward.*

---

[6] "I'm so cold"
"Nice to meet you, Cold."
"..."

The bad guy wins in this one.[7]

---

[7] "Thanks to this plot armour, I *can* keep getting away with it, losers!"

"Hey, Washington, we need you over here, buddy. We're about to write the Constitution into law. Got any last-minute changes you'd like to make? Now's your final chance!"

Let's expand that vocabulary a little, shall we?

Pick fifteen words out at random from *Urban Dictionary*[8] and work them into a short story.

---

[8] A personal favourite—*bootybrows*: "the creases between a woman's booty and her legs."

You've always thought that you were born into the wrong generation. Now, it's your time to prove it.

While writing your twentieth YouTube comment for the night, you unwittingly activated a temporal rift and were sent back to your most cherished era in human history.

What now?

Write a chapter[9] from a self-help book that isn't at all helpful.

---

[9] In the spirit of this prompt, it would be wrong of me to assist you here.

Deep in the bowels of your local Hot Topic, you find a bitchin' skull ring that reads *GYGES* on the inside. Probably an indie band or something. As you're playing around with it, you discover that twisting it clockwise grants you the ability to turn invisible.

How do you abuse your newfound power?

You've been going steady with your beau for two months. When they finally decide to invite you to a family gathering to meet their parents, you're ecstatic. That is, until you arrive and you see that her mother and father are the older couple you slept with back when you were sorting out your sexuality...

Write a free verse poem[10]
about the perfect partner
you'll realistically never get.[11]

---

[10] This is poetry without any fixed form. No mandatory rhymes, no mandatory metre, no mandatory syllable or line limits. Basically, anything goes. I know—so helpful.

[11] I'll start: *damn you fine*
like fine wine
why won't you
be mine?

It's 1912. You're chillin' at a cafe in Vienna when a serious, artsy-looking type bumps into you. "*Verzeihung,*" he says. When you look into his eyes, you notice the passion behind them. You also notice how good he would look with a toothbrush moustache.

You decide to invite him to sit with you...

Greasers, skinheads, hipsters, chavs—every era has its oh-so-punchable "non-conformists" to deal with.

But who will the 2020's have…?

Did you hear? A gang of interns from the office have started a fight club in one of the abandoned factories on the far side of town. The first rule of this fight club: everyone must be naked.[12]

---

[12] The second rule of this fight club: everyone must be naked.

Your character is a translator but is unable to understand, or translate, anything. This has interesting implications at this year's G20 Summit...

Twenty years ago, as a broke-ass college student who just wanted to buy a little booze and some Oreos, you sold your eggs[13] for some extra cash. You'd long forgotten about this until, one day, as you're coming home from work, you see a crowd of people standing on your lawn, and they're all holding baby pictures of themselves…

---

[13] Boys: semen. Naturally.

After taking five hits of DMT,[14] you've hit an entirely new plane of existence. Suddenly, the secrets of the universe reveal themselves to you. And you're not impressed. Why?

---

[14] N,N-Dimethyltryptamine. The "spirit molecule." Terrence McKenna took so much of it over the course of his life he invented a new super-strain of hippie.

Rebecca felt his powerful arms envelop her. She could hardly stop herself from gasping when her torso touched his chiseled abs. It was all happening so fast. If she didn't create some distance now, she'd lose herself in writing a Harlequin-style romance scene.[15]

---

[15] Just think of those novels you see in line at the grocery store—*His Majesty's Staff*, *The Cowboy's Daughter's Friend*, and the like.

Oedipus Complex?[16]
Oedipus Complex.[17]

---

[16] Your character wants to fuck their mom?
[17] Your character wants to fuck their mom.

To spite all the filthy plebeians out there, write a story crammed with the longest sentences and the most pretentious diction you can think of.

Nerds fidget with their pocket protectors; blonde bimbos reapply their make-up mid-class; jocks roam the hallways stuffing unsuspecting students into lockers; bad boys skip class to smoke cigarettes and wrestle with their latent self-esteem issues.

Such is life at Cliché High.

The Devil has been living a pretty comfortable life on earth—avoiding taxes, cheating at Go Fish, enjoying his very own brand of three-way.[18] That all changes when a rival arrives to usurp his role as king of the deplorables...

---

[18] ;)

Lo! Fair maiden, I have come to court thee. Mind not my cold sore![19]

---

[19] Write a story in which your main character is an archetypal, neckbeard-growing "good guy" (or girl!)

So *Harry Potter*[20] erotica exists. I'm not kidding. What's that? You'd kinda, maybe, like to try your hand at writing some, too? It's totally not 'cause you're into that sort of thing, though. I get it.

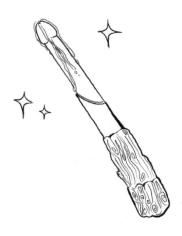

---

[20] Remember that old series about the wizard boy with the lightning bolt scar? No? Well, it's kind of niche stuff.

James Dean didn't get
smooshed by a truck;
Jimi Hendrix didn't puke
himself to death; Kurt Cobain
didn't try target practice in his
Seattle home; Marilyn Monroe
didn't die from losing her looks.

Where are they now?

Write a story[21] that includes the following line:

"As far as sex robots go, she was actually quite a skilled lover."

---

[21] Like any good story, it may take the following theoretical form:
exposition > rising action > climax > refractory period > pull-out

Through careful manipulation and a bit of luck, you've managed to establish yourself as the charismatic and holy leader of your own cult.

Tell us the story of what you had to do (and who you had to kill) to get this far.

They say that with your looks, your charm, your grace, you could be the next big Hollywood star. They've invited you down to the studio to talk about a role that you'd be perfect for. The receptionist leads you into an office and tells you to take a seat on the couch. A few minutes later, a powerful Hollywood executive tells you they'll make you a star.

If you take off your pants…

Write a haiku[22] about how fucking annoying nature is.

---

[22] Recall that funny little Japanese form teachers taught you in elementary school. Use the ol' 5-7-5 structure, or if you're feeling experimental, go shorter. Example: *spring morning—*
> *I challenge the woodpecker*
> *to a scrap*

Stephen King?

More like Stephen *Queen*.[23]

---

[23] A drag queen thriller? Bonus points if you can fit in a death drop.

Holy cow!

Your pet has developed the ability to talk. You've always wanted this. But now that you can properly communicate with each other, you realize your pet's a bit of a homophobic dick…

Write a note to your past or future self[24] detailing the few ways in which you have succeeded and the many, many ways in which you have let yourself down over the years.

---

[24] Who are we kidding? It's you. You might as well do both.

48

The evil Dr. Baby Boomer is at it again. He's poisoned the city's supply of craft beer in an attempt to rid the area of Millennials. You, a well-meaning, totally-not-anthropomorphic-bat-like vigilante might be able to save everyone—but first, you'll need to infiltrate his hidden lair.[25]

---

[25] It's *totally* not Applebee's.

Thanks to that sadistic Cupid, you've somehow managed to fall in love with the person you loathe most in this world.

Describe your third date and how much you enjoyed hate-fucking this particular individual.

Dude, like, isn't life, like, totally...crazy sometimes...? Yeah. I'd, like, totally like you to write out a stoner's inner...[26] uh, monologue[27] or whatever. Now watch me hit this chop.

---

[26] ???

[27] That thing when, like, the character thinks a lot or something. And then they say it to themselves. Yeah.

Dear Lord…

The Jehovah's Witnesses
are at your family's front
door, and they've got your
grandma under their spell!

It's not going to be an easy
fight. You're going to have to
cuss them out so hard they let
her go and never return.

Write a speech that gives 'em
the hell those cunts deserve!

You've got this little *deficiency*. A quirk, really. Whenever you hear a crying baby, you turn into a homicidal maniac. It's usually nothing serious. You hide it well.

However, today might be a bit of a challenge—you're about to babysit your sister's kid. Just how do you avoid killing her little bundle of joy?

Describe your first gay experience, even if you've never had, nor wanted, one.

You discover, in secret, a pill that for two hours at a time ratchets your IQ up to 400.

What havoc do you wreak on the world with your impressive intellect?[28]

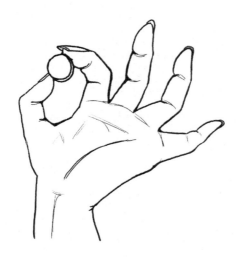

---

[28] Yes, yes—this is the plot of *Limitless*. I'm stealing the idea. So what?

Netflix has made the mistake of issuing you a blank cheque to write them their next hit show. They want a full outline of the first episode by next Tuesday, complete with character descriptions, plotline, and sample dialogue. Their only stipulation: "complete diversity"[29] —oh, and a little nudity

---

[29] Every character must be unique in age, race, and gender.

Minimalism.
No adjectives.
Story.
Go.[30]

Your Uber driver likes to talk. *A lot*. The GPS says that your trip is going to take forty minutes.

Describe the personal fucking hell you're in.

Step aside, AIDS—there's a new sheriff in town, and its name is Hyper Gonorrhea. Describe what it looks like in agonizing detail.

Warts and all.

Write a murder mystery where your protagonist —a sailor-mouthed graduate of the Jacques Clouseau School for Detectives— bumbles their way through the climax of another glaringly obvious case.[31]

---

[31] Bonus: make their language reek of that dreadful *American* French accent.

You wake up naked in Bangkok with a nasty headache. Your motel room is trashed, and your travel buddies are nowhere to be seen. Oh, and you're missing a kidney. In true *Hangover* fashion, piece together your night and tell the story in reverse.

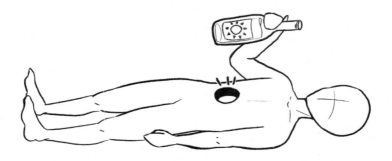

Your mixtape is *lit af* if you do say so yourself. There's no way this won't kill it on SoundCloud. Break us off a little sample of the lyrics, won't you?[32]

(Bonus: record it!)

---

[32] If you need a little inspiration, take some time to listen to the eternally graceful lyricism of Lil B, Lil Yachty, or any of the other infamous Lils.

Your hero is the tallest, veiniest, sleaziest, square-jawiest Chad around. His name? Toxic Masculinity Man.

Your publisher wants the first chapter of his (mis)adventures before the end of the day.

A chemist friend of yours tells you she's invented a new type of drug. She's not sure what it does yet, but she knows you're open-minded enough to try it. Her only advice: don't, under *any* circumstances, go out in public.

Predictably, you do.

Compose a fourteen-line, iambic pentameter[33] poem with an ABBAABBA CDDCDD rhyme scheme[34] about your love of hardcore porn. Show us how it's done, bard!

---

[33] We know this one now!

[34] A neat little arrangement for your rhymes. The final word of each line is assigned an alphabetic value based on its sonic properties. All rhyming words fall under the same letter. I'll give you a little taste:

My love! How wretched a husband I am (A)
Without thy feet at hand to squeeze this life, (B)
Without thy countenance with beauty rife— (B)
The sinful man without his cherished clam! (A)

Provide a vague, poorly thought-out synopsis of your favourite film.[35]

---

[35] "Oh, *Star Wars*? Yeah, uh, it's about a dude who goes to space to kill his black, asthmatic dad. So, in the opening scene…"

They're everywhere—soy latte-sipping, manbun-sporting, dungaree-loving hipsters. There isn't a person at this damned dinner party that isn't currently living solely off of legumes. After the third "Oh, so you haven't read *The Accumulation of Capital*?" you decide to fight back. You are determined to out-hipster everyone in the room.

Where do you begin?

After getting hit by a speeding truck, you wake up in a world modeled after Medieval Europe fantasy shows. Overhead, the voice of what seems like a fairy can be heard saying, "Hey, asshole! Wake up. I'm your personal guide. Welcome to Reichstaddenshlafen, land of the giant feminists."

Begin your story with the following paragraph:

"Occasionally, I pay two prostitutes—Cindy, a stretchmark-wielding mother of two, and Khalish, a hefty Malaysian man of at least forty years—to lie beside me in bed."

there's a crinkle of pity
between the
you're a nice guy
and the
you'll find someone else
that leads me to believe
this
was inevitable

— the left behind [36]

---

[36] Please write your own Rupi Kaur-style free verse
"Instapoem." Make sure to riddle it with clichés and
run-of-the-mill phrasing. Oh, and don't forget to
include a doodle!

Honestly, I'm feeling a bit too lazy to write a prompt for you at this very moment.

Why don't you come up with your own while daddy goes and powders his nose?

Tell, don't show.[37]

---

[37] Commit the cardinal sin of writing. Over and over and over again. You know you want to.

Your character is a method actor doing research for their next role. To prepare, they join a group for "Empowered Vegans"[38] on VeggieConnection.com. But this turns out to be more than your character bargained for when they attend the club's secret initiation ceremony…

---

[38] "We're lean, we're mean—get used to it!"

Think back to the last time you got bullied in school. Write that bastard or bitch a detailed letter,[39] letting them know you haven't forgotten what they did, and how, one day, when they're least expecting it, you're going to get your sweet revenge.

---

[39] Remember those paper rectangles that used to arrive through that weird hole in your front door?

Your perverted professor has asked you to write a paper on #bigdickenergy.[40]

Wanting to get a passing grade, you oblige...

You've just been given an N-Word pass.[41]

---

[41] Come on, it's not like you have any black friends who'll get upset.

Nothing induces panic quite like sending your mother an expertly-edited, filter-covered, high-resolution picture of your genitals. What's that? That's exactly what you just did?

Guess you're going to have to go downstairs and address this.

We all need a little bit of death in our lives—and so do our stories.

Write a one-page story in which *every* character dies.

(Bonus: kill the narrator.[42])

(Bonus-bonus: kill the third-person omniscient narrator![43])

---

[42] That guy or girl or extraterrestrial foot-fetishist who tells the story.

[43] That guy or girl or extraterrestrial foot-fetishist who tells the story and can see into each of the characters' innermost thoughts.

Remember that time you butt-dialed your boss by accident, and they could hear you furiously masturbating to hentai porn?

It's time to tell the world your side of the story.

As the result of much petitioning, the U.N. has just recognized emojis as an official world language. To celebrate this momentous decision, they would like you, the world's greatest emoji-user,[44] to write an official press release for the citizens of the world. Feel free to use your emojination.[45]

---

[44] "Emojer," if you will.
[45] If you want to be a real kiss-ass, write the whole thing in emojis.

You made the mistake of asking a hairless, legless, pet rat-having homeless man his life story. What you got in response was grosser— and, strangely, more erotic— than you could have ever believed…

Make like Chuck Palahniuk[46] and write an account of what it felt like, looked like—hell, what it smelled like—to exact justice on the dipshit that dared to cut you off during your morning commute yesterday.

Free verse is out.
Freer verse is in.[47]

---

[47] Show everyone what post-post-postmodernism is all about!

Between the middle-aged winos, farmers' market posts,[48] protein powder ads, and constant updates from your successful friends, your social media newsfeed is a goddamn disaster. Write your story of retribution as you go all *Punisher* on your friend list and purge it the old-fashioned way.

---

[48] We get it, Janet— apple pie's *such* a cool treat to eat on a summer's day.

In the style of your preferred writer, use dramatic dialogue[49] to detail a conversation between you and a very persistent, very fucking annoying customer service hotline representative.

---

[49] A form you've probably seen in a play. You have read a play before, yes? (Don't worry—plays are stupid.)

The year is 2045.

After a long day at Mega Corporation #6, your character has just walked in on their digital lover doing the pixel pump with someone else.

How do they cope with this digital cucking?

Write an account of the oft-forgotten first female conqueror's feats. Set these exploits in any time period you like.[50]

---

[50] 4000 BC, 5 AD, Whenever the fuck Scientologists think Xenu was doin' his thing on earth. Is her army a band of bikini-clad warriors from the Western Caucasus? Perhaps a gaggle of Amazonians battling the Conquistadors?

We love juxtaposition, don't we? Literature's full of that shit. That's why you're going to write a story set in high society[51] wherein all of the characters speak as if they're preteens using MSN Messenger in 2007.[52]

---

[51] Upper crust Victorian England? A palace? Chuck-E-Cheese?

[52] *lawl XD ur so funny*
dude stephanie is soooo hot i cant beleive it
wat did u just say 2 me u fukin idiot ill kill ur cat

Write a teacher/student romance set in your school's Special Ed. Department.[53]

---

[53] You bought this book. You want this.

Wanna write a kids' book? Of course you do. Instead of retreading the same old boring narratives, why not write the origin story of GiGi, the super gay unicorn who loves sucking horn? Today, in your fantasy world, he goes to a bath house…

There's nothing civilized about our modern society. So, it's time for you to start your own. You've studied Plato; you've read Machiavelli; you've watched *Real World: Las Vegas*. You know how these things work.

Describe this paradise on earth in three paragraphs.

Imagine you're the president of the United States. You're in the Oval Office, in a highly important meeting. But you have *un-fucking-believable* diarrhea.

Draft a short memo to your chief-of-staff on how you plan on getting out of the meeting without giving away your explosive secret.

Write the first act of a romantic comedy about a woman and her hilarious—and completely illegal—love of dead bodies.[54]

---

[54] "Coming this summer: a fun-filled romp about one woman's quest to find love...with a cadaver!"

Well, you missed almost all of your grandpa's birthday. But don't worry—you arrive right at the end, dressed as a clown, reeking of urine, and missing two teeth. Where have you been, Pagliacci?

Tell a story using copious amounts of footnotes[55] throughout to clarify or confuse.

---

[55] Hey! Here's your chance to do what I'm doing.

No Nut November. Day 3. The patient appears to be experiencing mild delusions and increased heart rate. Earlier this morning, they could be heard saying they would "bust a nut so hard, sea levels will rise." At the sight, sound, or smell of any stimuli considered sexual, the patient may explode. You're the doctor on call.

What do you suggest?

We're goin' contemporary on this one.

Create a piece of flash fiction[56] in which the words *fuck*, *shit*, *bitch*, and *cunt* all appear at least five times each.

---

[56] A short short story, or, in essence, a short story for the supremely lazy.

Clark Kent is Superman.

Bruce Wayne is Batman.

Spider-Man is Tobey McGuire.

It seems everyone has an alter-ego within them.

Who's yours?[57]

---

[57] Would it happen to be Big Stomach (Wo)Man, terrorizer of all-you-can-eat buffets everywhere?

You know who gets a pretty bad rap? Judas. I mean, all he did was sell out the Lord's Boy to the Romans. No one ever takes the time to try to see things from *his* perspective. That's where you come in. Pen a journal entry[58] from the perspective of Judas immediately following the whole "crucifixion" incident.

[58] Remember when you used to write that "Dear Diary" shit late at night? That.

If you would please, spin a tale that climaxes with the line,

"…and that's how my happy ending made me sad."[59]

---

[59] I think we've all been there before.

Friends. Who needs 'em? That's what online forums are for. Imagine you've just logged on, fully prepared to launch into a massive rant about everything that pisses you off. Write it down. Vent that invective for as long as you want. Don't stop until you've cleansed yourself of every irritating thing you can think of. Feel better? You're welcome, cupcake.

Easily impressed by everything, your characters are over the moon when they arrive at their local Dollar Tree store.

Describe in embarrassing detail their $75 spending spree.

Everyone says they've been on at least one awful date before, be it with Jeffrey, the *Star Trek* nerd from your Math class, or Jessica, the legally stupid receptionist from the office, or Alina, the foreign beauty who *definitely* roofied you at some point in the night. Surely, though, there is a date out there that may rightly be considered the worst of all time…

Show those Hollywood hacks what's up and write a scene from a screenplay positively riddled with unfilmable subjects.[60]

---

[60] Make *120 Days of Sodom* look like an episode of *Teletubbies*.

For this next prompt (sing. noun), you're going to write (verb) a *Mad Lib*[61] (proper noun) about what it's like to navigate the perfect (adj.) hell (noun) that is getting your period. Get a friend (or enemy) to fill it out!

---

[61] Plz don't sue. Thx!

Give me your best poverty meal recipe.[62]

I really want to know what to pair my boxed wine with.

---

[62] Without proper measurements and directions, how will I ever learn how to make mustard nachos?

Rewrite the first ten pages of
The Bible.[63]

Make sure to introduce the
character of Kanye West
on page 2.

---

[63] A.K.A. *The Good Book, The Word of God,*
That Thing Grandpa Keeps Saying I Need.

Charm can go a long way— but so can logic.

Write a formal argument in which you justify a thoroughly immoral act.[64]

---

[64] Don't forget to BuRN aFtEr WrItINg.

Oozing testosterone and sporting the most bitchin' aviators around, your leather-clad, cocaine-fueled protagonist is everything an 80's action hero should be. He's got the muscle, he's got the look, but he also happens to be afflicted with severe social anxiety because of the size—or lack thereof—of his micropenis.

It drives people mad when you switch tenses all the time, doesn't it? And we love to drive people mad, don't we? Write an advertisement for birth control pills in which each sentence features a different verb tense.[65]

---

[65] If you're an absolute sicko and actually *like* grammar, feel free to jump around between specific tenses. If you're a normal person, just stick to hopping between general timeframes.

You've found yourself in some type of *Hot Tub Time Machine*-esque madness, and have managed to enter the body of your twelve-year-old self.[66]

What—or whom—do you do first?

---

[66] Phrasing!

Write a fairy-tale that ends
with the line,

"And from that day on, white
people left us alone."

In an attempt to escape the friend zone, you kidnap your would-be partner. This has unexpected consequences when, five minutes in, you discover that they are *impossibly* clingy…

Your character has been up for 72 hours. Fun!

In a stream-of-consciousness[67] live feed, recount what they've been up to.

---

[67] A writing style meant to mimic thought. There are essentially no rules. Just do whatever the fuck you want. If you want to add an errant capital letter, or number, into your sentence jUst do 1t.

You love your goth partner. They've got a pentagram tattooed around their butthole, a couple rat fetuses on their bookshelf, and, you suspect, a host of unresolved daddy issues. Lately, they've been deathly afraid of garlic. If you didn't know any better, you'd think you were dating a twenty-first century vampire or something… Nah, there's no way. Right?

You, the first King of Garbage Island[68] conquered the plains of plastic and ushered in an era of prosperity for all the sea creatures in the area. What songs do the pelican poets now sing in your honour?

---

[68] You're like Aqua-man, but surrounded by plastic water bottles.

Life as a door-to-door salesperson blows. Following yet another disastrous attempt to sell flimsy tableware to seniors, you decide you've had enough. You're going to use the skills you've gained and your nauseatingly positive can-do attitude to sell cocaine instead.[69]

---

[69] "Well, hiya there, cracked-out Craig! Care to try some of the world's finest Bolivian marching powder? It'll knock your blood-stained socks off. I guarantee it!"

You're up on the stand. The judge is utterly disgusted with you. Your mother won't even look your way. With the threat of unwanted penitentiary penetration looming above you, you begin your defence...

Your defence didn't go so well. You've been sent to the big house, and your new cellmate looks like the frisky type. But a couple of iron bars aren't going to hold you back. You've already started planning the most daring prison escape in history. You have at your disposal a mirror, a shiv, two matches, and a deceptively charming smile. Show us how it's done, Andy Dufresne.

It's time to give birth to your own Frankenstein's Monster.[70]

Mix together the plots of your five favourite books and write the first chapter of your literary abomination.

---

[70] No, before you get ahead of yourself, this isn't a poop joke. Grow up.

Janey leads a relatively normal life. She works, attends night school, enjoys the occasional bender. Only there's one thing that makes her unique: her heart stops if she doesn't pleasure herself every five minutes.

This funeral should be fun.

I wish I could go off the grid. Man, it sure would be nice to spend some time off the grid, y'know? Off-the-grid living sure—

Christ! Just go off the grid already. But do it *Naked and Afraid*[71] style, and keep a journal to capture all your delicious suffering.

---

[71] This is going to be re-e-e-al tough if you're one of those bizarre "never-nudes."

Pandemonium breaks loose when you let a group of Twitch live-stream viewers dictate how to live your life for the next twenty-four hours. Just how did they get you chained up in Leonardo DiCaprio's basement…?

Let's start at the beginning.

Some disturbing news is coming out of the East End. All of those goldfish you thought you'd killed out of neglect throughout your childhood have banded together in the sewers of your city. And now they want retribution.

Write a short science fiction story without any science. Or fiction.

What? Our time together is up already? It can't be! Well, if you must go, why don't we leave things off on a positive note? Write me the most kick-ass suicide note anyone's ever read. Bare your soul![72] And don't give me any of that woe-is-me bullshit!

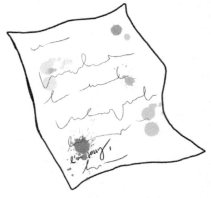

---

[72] Provided, of course, that you still have one after reading this book.

Get in Touch
Send your wildest responses to
promptsgonewild@gmail.com

Or submit them through **promptsgonewild.com**
for a chance to be featured on the website and
social media.

DM me on Instagram or Twitter **@promptsgonewild**

And whether you loved or hated the book,
let me know by dropping a review online!

#promptsgonewild

Acknowledgements
Thanks to Malcolm Croft, Matt Windsor, and my
ex-Tinder-fling-turned-illustrator, @lycheetinii

Printed in Great Britain
by Amazon

28164314R00076